MW01435361

LAKE OF TWO MOUNTAINS

>>

LAKE OF TWO MOUNTAINS

››

ARLEEN PARÉ

BRICK BOOKS

LIBRARY AND ARCHIVES CANADA CATALOGUING IN PUBLICATION

Paré, Arleen, author
    Lake of two mountains / Arleen Paré.

ISBN 978-1-926829-87-6 (pbk.)

    I. Title.

PS8631.A7425L35 2014   C811'.6   C2013-907368-X

Copyright © Arleen Paré 2014.
Third Printing – December 2014

We acknowledge the Canada Council for the Arts, and the Ontario Arts Council for their support of our publishing program.

This book is set in FF Scala, Designed by Martin Majoor and released by FontFont in 1991.
Cover image, design and layout by Cheryl Dipede.

The author photo was taken by Ryan Rock.
Printed and bound by Sunville Printco Inc.

BRICK BOOKS
431 Boler Road, Box 20081
London, Ontario N6K 4G6
www.brickbooks.ca

For my sister, Donna, who knows the water lilies that grow under the bridge.

CONTENTS

Distance Closing In » 5
More » 6
Becoming Lake » 7
Alnöitic Rock » 9
Under Influence » 10
Summer House Revisited » 11
Figments » 13
How Fast a Life » 14
Summer » 15
Map of the Lake » 17
Monastic Life 1 » 21
Monastic Life 2 » 22
Monastic Life 3 » 23
Call and Response » 24
How Own a Lake » 27
Kanesatake » 29
Impermanence » 31
Whether Wind » 32
Monastic Life 4 » 34
Monastic Life 5 » 35
Whose Lake? » 36
Lake 1 » 38

Religious Life ›› 39
Monastic Life 6 ›› 40
Dad before Lake ›› 41
Swimming under the Overhead Fixture ›› 42
Dad in the Lake ›› 44
Older Aunt ›› 45
Treading Water ›› 46
Uncle Bobby ›› 47
To Oka ›› 48
How Belong ›› 50
How Mend the Years ›› 51
Angelwings ›› 52
Frère Gabriel Crosses the Lake ›› 53
Frère Gabriel's Life 1 ›› 54
Frère Gabriel's Life 2 ›› 55
Frère Gabriel's Life 3 ›› 56
Armies of Frogs ›› 57
Oka Crisis ›› 59
Northern Gate ›› 62
L'Île-Cadieux ›› 63
Walking the Island Road after Dinner ›› 64
Frère Gabriel's Life 4 ›› 65
Frère Gabriel's Life 5 ›› 66
When Heat Falls ›› 67
Cardinals, Crows ›› 68
Lake 2 ›› 69

Ghosts Moving in Forested Shade ›› 70
Summer Ends ›› 71
Things Change ›› 72
Last Day ›› 73
Monastic Life 7 ›› 75
Monastic Lake ›› 76
What's Under ›› 77
Eight Miles to the Centre ›› 78
Sun Going Down ›› 79

Acknowledgements ›› 81
Biographical Note ›› 83

All that we love, we try to memorize.
—*Chase Twichell*

DISTANCE CLOSING IN

flint-dark far-off
sky on the move across the lake
slant sheets closing in

sky collapsing from its bowl
shoreline waiting   taut
stones dark as plums

closer   future
flinging itself backwards
water now stippling thin waterskin

shallows pummelled   the world
hisses with rain   iron-blue smell
and pewter light ringing

MORE

vision doubles
the lake's surface calmed
trees displaying roots into roots
their upside-down selves

tree selves downside-up
in the water where their roots
touch their roots   a surfeit of calm
redoubles the lake

BECOMING LAKE

Start early. Pleistocene.
3 a.m. Let the Laurentide Ice Shield
wrench surface snow, blast
great pans of pale frozen foam.
Thunder out. Cacophony of cold,
glacial-scour. Scoop a basin
five miles across.

Let the bowl corrugate.
                Beneath the plain,
concavitate in slow ragged folds.
Sink potholes. Shove mountain tops
from below stony roots. Spall,
brinell, press walls whipped with sleet.
Penance the ice. Endure
the murk, the minutes, millennia.

Empty out the salt sea.

Watersheds, drains,
daily rains gelatinate the sky.

                    Conjure blue then,
olive-green, brown, streaks of violet gold,
precipitation's long sombre hush. Rubble,
river mouth, almighty mud.

All things fall away, sink
into brokenness.

                        Finally,
ripple-scum and shore fog, water
grey-pocked – but moving,
currents, then caps of white,
the lake's silver face
scudded with wind.

ALNÖITIC ROCK

Fits (this uncertain rock) into your hollowed hand.

Muskrat-skull rock, mauved in places as if bled.

Hole-pocked fossil rock. A cipher. Left behind

when ice plates receded. Continental sheets.

Ice on the move. Leaving what cannot cleave.

Topographies herded flat, wide as the weft of caribou hooves.

Hoof-heavy plumb of time (here and Baffin Island only).

Or volcano-spewed, dropped from the sky.

Primordial cool, old questions weight in your palm.

UNDER INFLUENCE

Jack-in-the-pulpit, brown-streaked and hooded,
preaches to primeval ferns.
Poison ivy inveigles
these low-lying woods.
                                  The influence
of wild-carrot heads, road-side
orange hawkweed, mulberry,
milkweed, purple vetch. Maple-tree light
beguiles the liquid afternoon air, leaches
logic, riffles the grey leather beech.

The past develops under water,
film fixing invisible forms
the way dreams reveal
what was already there.

Bullfrogs horn the first part of night,
half in, half out of the lake;
each domed note baritones
the last, migrations of sound.

The past arranges itself
under duress. Loneliness leaves
its wet-animal print, darker on dark.
Under the influence,
the weight of the land, sleight
of wave-length configures a life.

SUMMER HOUSE REVISITED

A notice on your house (which is not
yours anymore): *Avis municipal, le permit* . . . .
It's hard to know what comes next.
                    Your sister reads French,
but the print is small, the notice long,
and the day rockets by. In front, beyond the low wall,
wind pitches the lake.

Clapboard, tall as a sail, the house
billowed in summer, but in winter
it measured its breath,
pooled silence in porcelain bowls,
stashed haircombs, clamshells under the eaves.

Before that sign appeared,
                    the past had no end.

No one is home. You peek through the dark windows.
Who lives here now
means nothing to you.

Only the lake remains real, its abandonments
slow as the stars. The path to the lake
rucks over with sedges, gooseberries,
your dead aunt's *muguets de bois*.
The water that leaks from your palm
still smells like a cold silver spoon.

A boat (not your boat)
rocks on the white water.
Shore grasses sharpen the air,
scythe the wind as it blows off the fetch.

FIGMENTS

God and molecules, nuclei and neutrinos:
you're told certain uncertain things.

Told this is your mother,
whose coffined face you don't know,
whose dress is a dress she'd never have owned.

If you could, you'd live below theory, subatomic
notions floating unseen. Helixed webs,
beyond life's unparseable range.

You'd believe in spiders, though they too
occupy their own theoried world.
On ceilings, unfalling, they attach, reattach,
rappelling. Their silks
unconcerned with what gravity can do.

Your mother sat you, as a baby, in the shallows,
the lake licking your spine.
Her face then was all you needed to know.

There's a photograph. Part of the web.
Everything beginning that moment,
untheoried, exposed.

HOW FAST A LIFE

You stood at the end
of the wharf, you and your sister.
Cautious. In handfuls, your mother's ashes
catching the wind,
landing on the lake's surface.
End of June, wind
lifted your hair.

                  Which is how
it might have been.

                  The lake is not
a lake, only a bulge in the river;
the two mountains, only hills.

Your mother spent her summers here.
She knew how fast
a storm surged. Ricocheted across water
from the far-off north shore.
Darkness catapulting.
        When it came, the air turned
electric. Even the house, chill
as an icebox,
every light going out.

SUMMER

                starts when the Dodge
downshifts   drifts down the path
onto thin tufted grass
                   sinks into loose
shifting soil settles
                    in sandiness

                the small hopeless lawn
aprons the south side of the house
struggles towards its own rootedness
hunts for sunlight
through holes in the deciduous haunt

two stumps   one stunted spirea in new pointed leaf
startled now
by car doors which slam
first one   then the other

                 summer starts
when island air curls on girls'
freckled cheeks   feckless bare legs

 starts when the screen door unlatches
and the thick door behind
creaks its wood-swollen groan
releasing odours of a weather-sealed house
double-windowed for months
caulked against cold

as if cold could be stopped
it iced the lake twenty feet down
froze every sturgeon
one fish at a time

                summer starts
up the staircase   iron beds
guarding the past   last year's swimsuits
hanging
ghost torsos noosed on their hooks
stretched overlong

summer last   on the bottom
of the unplumbed blue tub   spider legs   moth wings
drained into otherness
last year's ant traps
shadflies   mosquitoes   houseflies in husks
their wire-thin legs curling in

summer starts
                from the second-floor window
overlooking the lake
the world open-handed   opening
into each summer gone
                each summer beginning
in shore light
stretching beyond the dark line of pines

MAP OF THE LAKE

Draw the map three feet long, maybe four –
but not wide – on paper strong enough
to box-pleat left to right, store in a drawer.
Make it nautical, but add some terrain.

Use coloured pencils, otherwise coloured felt pens.
Base the map loosely
on *Oceans and Fisheries, Map 1500*.

                                    Begin at page bottom,
outlining an island shaped like a feather, stemmed
to the lake's southern shore.

Pencil then to the left, curving the shoreline west
from the stem. Use the blue. The lake
is usually brown but no one believes
a brown lake.
This is a map, not real life.

Draw rocks on the shore.
In places indicate short stretches of sand.
Indicate a tiny islet
directly in front of the feather-island's
middle-north shore. Draw six maple trees there.
Bend them from the waist to the east
as though the trees are in prayer.

Fashion the old-fashioned symbol –
wind-face with puffed cheeks – in the map's
upper left. The wind blows from the west
most days of the year.

Scallop the lake's edge to the left and up. The lake's shape,
a long ragged stretch –
imagine the shape of a cloud:
a bird with broad wings
and no head; or a pelvis, wide-hipped;
or a snake having swallowed a hawk.

Mid-left, which is west, break the line
at the place where the river runs in, the place
where twin ferries, to and from Oka,
pass each other from six in the morning
till midnight
when the service shuts down.
Draw the two ferries – flat barges –
in red and in white. Draw fourteen cars
on each barge.

                  To the south,
at the map's bottom left, print "Hudson."
Pencil in a fine horse and a rider in boots.

To the north, print "Oka."
                        Here, draw a church.
Use the silver. The steeple is tall. Indicate bells,
make them ring but only on Thursday and Sunday
when Masses are held. Inside the church
draw a painted-wood saint, a young Mohawk girl,
or maybe Huron, who is said to heal rifts.
The rest of the time the church locks its doors.
So close the doors – draw their groan
and the slam. Draw the lock. Label the church

"St. Francis of Assisi." Once Sulpician,
but that church burned down.

The rift in the line is where the river debouches;
it doesn't need healing. Label it "The Ottawa."
Its water is brown, but again choose the blue.

Colour the lake's two eponymous mountains.
The sun used to slip behind them at eight, but who knows
what time it is now. This is a map;
maps change all the time.

Continue the shoreline along the top of the page.
This shoreline is Oka.
Show the settlement called Kanesatake,
pine trees, a graveyard, some hills. Use the dark green.
Fashion a flag, red, yellow and black, to remember
the Crisis two decades ago. Bow your head.
Extend a long line to project past the golf course,
the town, into the beach's pale sand.
                                                            To the right
show the place where the monastery stands.
Use middle grey. Draw the silence in blue – darker –
now that the monks are all gone.

                                          Wiggle light blue
to the right, past Pointe-Calumet and Ste.-Marthe-sur-le-Lac.
Break the line. Here the water runs out.
Break the line, once again, between L'Île-aux-Tourtes
and Pointe Abbote. A bridge there leads to the highway.
Use the light grey.
Trains cross a parallel bridge: frame trestles and arches.

Draw a freight train, draw the long lonely sound
of boxcars calling to night.

Sketch twenty small islets, maybe more, using leaf green.
Hook up the blue line back at the feather's short stem,
south of the island: L'Île-Cadieux.
Place a white clapboard house
at the island's mid-section
facing north to Oka's broad beach five miles away,
the pinery, the former two hundred monks.
Pitch its roof to a peak. Pierce the house
with four rectangle windows. Make them look out
over the lake. Use the black.
Mark the place: "You are here."

MONASTIC LIFE 1

It is exterior, what can be seen, touched, not just what adjoins the pure mind. Trappist buildings, granite-stoned, black and stern-grey, in the midst of bramble and trees. Belonging to this place, sanctuary, for however long the body will last.

It is the maze of outbuildings: one marble-slabbed for white Oka cheese; one filled with barrels of apples rosy as Our Lady's stiff plaster lips. One building to hide washtubs and lye. Hives. Barns. And near the barns, coops for the chicken and eggs. Sheds where tapers hang their long fingers to dry. A gazebo not far from the lake.

It is the massive main building itself, which shelters pantries with shelves of gooseberry jams and mustards made from wild mushrooms. Benches and sills, halls, dormitories, single cells. A chapel lined with white pine. A refectory with seats for two hundred. Banks of cook stoves. Ceilings, heaven-high to heighten the quiet. Rooms for visits and rooms for prayer. A sewing room to repair torn wool. A room for the dead and for the families to story the dead.

It is summer heat, the lake to the south hugging sloped laps of shrubs, its loping length floating with monarchs and blackbirds with red-feathered wings. The rest, inconsequential, nothing of import on the shore far across. The thin sky there reflects only want.

MONASTIC LIFE 2

It is interior. Hidden in cochlea. Behind lenses, just under the skin. It is the sound of chair legs backing away from the table. Three times a day. The fragrance of beeswax. Soundless prayer. Morning mist, incense lifting from the censer's broad swing.
                      Not the censer. Not the convex of the
bells, silver-etched, angels and stars. Not twelve wheels of cheese or a hand held in the forge. Not the hammer or horse. Not white robes, hoods, tunics of wool. But the effect of it all. The bells' seduction. Geese rising from shore. Not the wafer, but the wafer's weight on the tongue, light as ash. Not the man, but the way a man disappears in the habit of all.

MONASTIC LIFE 3

It is confession. Inside: envy and anger, trespasses, how to forgive. It is prayer and the mother who still mourns her long-vanished son. It is God behind rib slats, God in the hollows of mouths. It is angels, feathers weighing down scapulas. Nightbodies flying through the solitude that sanctity can make. Alveoli-frilled gloriosa and clear tenor notes. It is waiting for the break-openness of clavicles. Snapping in two. Rat-scurry sounds become wings at the narrow night window. Wild roses twine round the spine. Bees colonize the innermost ear.

CALL AND RESPONSE

I.
The Canadian Shield calls to the fault
in Timiskaming Lake. The Shield shelters

more than half the land. The fault, tectonic,
replies with the Ottawa River, whose waters run east

and spread at the place of two mountains.
Becoming lake. In this way the lake is of lake,

song of song, Deux-Montagnes out of Timiskaming.
The lake there, at the two mountains, calls

to the trees near and around, riparian trees
on rocky shores and the terrestrials

within two miles of the shore. Perpetual loop.
One verse then the other. Connecting

trees to the sand, the orthic, melanic, brunisol soil,
tree canopies, consolations of climate.

The way birds in the morning define the new day,
call sunrise from night.

2.
         The trees call to each other their own
names: sugar maple, hickory, eastern white pine.

Black willow chants the alphabets of green ash.
Yellow birch calls to red maple, chokecherry to beech.

They bear multiple names: formal, scientific,
common French and the names that are Mohawk.

And no names at all. Their calls
travel through air, water, through earth,

sedges and shrubs, algae
and cumulus clouds. All conversing.

Rocks and black leeches. Sturgeon, green frogs.
Limestone and vascular plants.

3.
                How does the sky
reply when silver-backed leaves tug at the wind,

blocking the passage to sea?
                      Clouds ring with rain

and the lake lifts small pewter washes
                              in rows of applause.

What listens to sugar maples' clear amber flow?
Rays: yellow and cold.

Fine beads of drizzle
                      hiss the filigreed ice.

What answers flood cover drowning hickory knees?
Clay or silt. Till or clay loam. Sap in the spring.

4.
Sugar maple is always and in all places attentive,
alert for replies from the open terrain.

The soil, fine or sandy, alluvium,
measures the length of flood time in spring,

speaks a name to the climate,
the warmest in the whole province. Call

and response: a dominant tree, *Acer saccharum*,
a sweetness that humans tap into.

HOW OWN A LAKE

A child begins owning
                the lake,
its lifting haunt in morning,
its sun-slapped birds. Begins
to own the rud
that coats evening,
                        sunsets hinged
behind the gap to the west. Begins

owning the islet that floats offshore,
boulder-pinned.
                She upends smaller stones,
plucks innocent snails. She claims
the islet's frogs and the ribbits of frogs,
moves the stirring lumps.

                      Owns the waves
and the far shore that looses them. Owns
water lilies bobbing beneath the far-end bridge,
yards them out, lays them in layers
on the rowboat's wet floor.

She owns water weeds that yank at her feet,
tadpoles butting, which she collects, black leeches,
which she salts.

And the monastery across the lake,
which she can't see, does she own it as well?
And the reservation across the lake,
completely unknown?

The duck blind near the point, she claims.
And lapping sounds.
                        And darning needles
switching blue, and rapiers of grass,
the briny pong, the smart of slime that chokes
the small elbowed bay.

And the lake. The lake
                    begins owning
the child, carves its winged shape
into her young,
green-stick bones, into places there
where holiness will soak,
and a loneliness she can't hope to shake.

KANESATAKE

the reserve on the lake banners maple and oak
sumac   a warrior flag
the road through is knee-high grass-flanked

northward for miles only trees and grass moving
no people   no dogs

your car driving
nowhere you know
until rain speckles the windscreen

a sense of trespass   the threat
of a downpour
you decide to turn back

everything flashes by in reverse
rain-splattered signs   maples and oaks
Christmas lights at the ends of the driveways

hand-lettered signs   or neon signs blinking
eggs for sale fireworks cigarettes cigarettes
Tabac Chez Nous and *Best Butts   Mohawk Gas*

once a figure appeared   gas station to car
then a warning: *we don't collect taxes*
for any foreign government

and the flag   red yellow and black
the nine-hole golf course next door
only two cars on the road   a small truck
the shush   the wet road

not that you live here but
                        would you leave if you had to
                        (your life being trespass)
                        and where would you go?

to Ireland's south-west where your mother's people are from
or to Antrim where your father's father   or Glasgow
where your father was born
                        displacements and exile
this not being your people's original place

can you go back
to where
you never have been?

IMPERMANENCE

                    elm trees dead now
still fan-shape under your lids
silver-roofed barns blister your sight in sub-zero cold
a pharmaceutical plant
stands where a woodlot once grew
and the creek behind the McTavishes'
is now covered over with fill
the pussy willows
on the hill near the creek
ploughed under and gone

                    but the summertime lake
its vast runnelled sprawl
reluctant in late day to let anything go
your lips as a child turned delphinium blue
your knife-pleated fingers
pale as small fish

WHETHER WIND

> *I walk on ghosts / apparitional gatherings carry me along.*
> Don Domanski

the night you lost your parents   it was
evening   first   summer   maybe August
parts are missing
                the length of the shadows
the mileage from Fran's house
to yours   missing
           or never known
           how you got home
why the doors were all locked
darkness
inking inside and outside your body

you were nine
      but even your age
           or if that night
the bullfrogs made any sound   whether
your dead grandmother hovered
in front of   or behind
the outer screen door
the kitchen window streaked
                reflecting

you said good-bye   leaving Fran's house
light hanging by threads
you ran the road
evening wind picking up
        but even the wind

or if maple leaves bled to black   if trees
began hemming the road
or if you wore nothing at all
on your arms

you knew only the night   something lost
whether wind   or black leaves

whether you found them
                            or were found
whether either is true

MONASTIC LIFE 4

It resides with honeybees, rows of hives along wire fences to the west, each queen drowsing in the jellied centre of a world. Bless each queen, that she survives the freeze, that she recites sweet piping sounds in spring as icicles release the sun. Bless the orchard trees as they hold up their plain grey twigs. Fields of clover one day will levitate, hover in July's keening light. Bless the workers too, dull-huddled in their combs: that they remember flight, uncup their double wings against leftover cold. Bless each monk who dreams of honey, pantried light, stolen to illuminate dim winter shelves. They are praying for forgiveness. And for blossoms to burst April buds.

MONASTIC LIFE 5

It is liturgical. Worship, proper times of the day. One time, then another, in order, each time reaching. When one ends, thoughts of the next arise. Quotidian. Before collecting the milk, Matins. Before resting, Compline. Before reaching God, reaching out for God. Everyone becoming a saint. Before contemplating the miracle of clouds or of fish, the hour's office. To praise God. Who hovers over the ferns, over faces hooded in barns, the brown backs of cows. Life among maples. God in herringboned pine cones, in clams boring into the sand. Worshipping the wild horse-tailed sky. When wind rises. Snow falls. When sap varnishes the flanks of cold trees. Every season, God. And reaching out for God. Every hour passes ordained. In this place of yellow perch and bluegill, trillium and ribbon grass, all eyes know when to close. All eyes look at what they are looking for.

WHOSE LAKE?

My lake says the man
with the speedboat
because his uncle
once owned a camp at Rigaud where the river
breaks into the lake

God's lake says
Frère Gabriel because
he believes God owns
whatever He wants
and who wouldn't want this particular lake

My lake you say
and the lake of your sister
because your grandfather
and mother and aunts
and your uncle
once owned the white house up the road
and you stayed every summer
and swam every day
rain or shine

Our lake say the Mohawks
and the lake of our dead
because they lived
here or near enough here
and died here
if not from time immemorial
at least almost as long

My lake says the woman
who rents you the room
who owns the patio chairs
and the curved turquoise pool
and the long windy fore-shore
performing before you
and the house like a rock
or a deity
watching your backs

LAKE 1

The lake harbours no greed. Rain comes, the lake simply receives. Rain comes in spring, and the ice, in plates and in discs, moves east, leaving crust and a thick, ragged skirt. Grit that falls through, trail of a fox falling in. Everything is poor. Rain comes, and wind. Wind like a cousin, not always kind. Wind-scrub and wind-wash, rough play and tease. Wind drags the lake's floor, casts up what's past dying. Swollen boards from fish huts, rented in winter, towed onto the ice, bird wings, broken at shore, rotten fish. The lake has nothing to ask, its ear cupped. Its hearing fills with nothing but rain. Water rises. Herons shrug in rock hollows, frogs wallow deeper in mud. Floods well. Lake opens up, gleaming, a chalice brimmed to the lip.

RELIGIOUS LIFE

Daring move. The school is old, made of wood: one match would torch it to ground before lunch. Who'd save the children? Even now, old snow still shrinks their schoolyard. Splinters fester inside their pine desks. Each groaning stair, saddle-bowed. Still, God shoulders in – grade four, the last tractable age.

He sneaks in through catechism's call and response:
Who is God?
God is love.
How long is eternity?
However long it takes a dove's wing to wear away the marble-hard world.

God slips in at 2:30, brushing past the folds of Sister Zita's grey gown. His beard swirling dust. Through the Stations of the Cross, through His Son, He enters their stories, their grade-four adventures. The man's terrible gore, his thorn-tangled hair. Father and child, sufferings and wrongs.

Once a month, Sister Zita fire-drills a bucket of flames on the unsafe escape. God tends the flames. Day by day, He replaces black snow-melt with spring. The wolves at the chain links are flame-eyed with want.

MONASTIC LIFE 6

Silence colludes with shadow, pervasive blur that underhangs archways between granite walls. Walk, look at the feet. One boot, then the other. Note how clay dries in stiff clots, sculpts frills around heavy soles. Note the monk-shaped shadow falling from boot soles heading away from the sun. Silence lasts a lifetime. Life lived beneath, burrowed under the sky. Say nothing: think only of God. The last consolation. Silence enters the body; the body does not enter silence. Beseech the Holy Spirit to haunt the chiaroscuro of soul. Watch the soup fall from the ladle into white bowls. Eat the bread. Be grateful. And for the boots that keep to the path. Grateful. Look down at the feet.

DAD BEFORE LAKE

Before the ocean liner, *Transylvania:*
homing pigeons on the coal-scuttle roof,
pink and pearl grey, tin grey with rainbows,
and white with red feet:
Maggie and Nessie, Mrs. McWing.

Before Montreal: Mossend, west of Glasgow,
the old Bloch Hearn Yards on the Clyde where his father
slung sheets of hot steel, each one
the size of a bed. Family home,
a block from the pub.

Before the lake: Montreal, new,
and the French, Jamaicans and Jews.
The Protestants he already knew how to hate.

Before the lake: the Depression.
Not enough food or work. The wagon horse. Winter
on the treacherous ice.

Before my mother, he organized dances,
wore dress suits, lapels like dark folded kites.

After my mother: the lake.
He called the lake Shangri-La.

SWIMMING UNDER THE OVERHEAD FIXTURE

          in measured strokes   the crawl
right arm   then the left   head and backbone
aligned   head-pivot
synchronizing   drawn-back elbows
first one up   a piston
breathing in
breathing out
          then the other
all along the long hallway
two feet below
the stained plaster ceiling
no windows
          fingertips glancing against
the overhead fixture's
bevelled-glass rim
feet flutter-kicking   toes
grazing the wallpaper once
once kicking a framed watercolour
right off its nail
the end-stop   faraway door
unopened   maybe sealed
          each stroke defying
the unfluid laws of aerodynamics
the air   warm and unwet
somehow buoys the methodical flight
arms tire then
a careful stroke-switch to the breast
head down   legs frogged
and push   push again

the continuous risk of the height
a thin carpet runner on the far-below floor
headroom capped   cobwebs
and the small distant door
still unopened   unmoved

DAD IN THE LAKE

Lewd, his close-fitting jersey-knit
swimsuit, della robbia blue, drawstring
at his waist, dark hair coiled on his chest,
his sinewy thighs,
his knees, small onions, ivory-hued.

His pale feet, unprotected, rock him
down to the edge. And in. He stumbles
on the slip of stones, almost pitches,
before the shallows knee-deepen,
water slapping into his lap.

                    Lowering now,
body to neck, he delivers himself
to the lake, hands finning below his raised chin.
In front of the dock, paddling
one direction, then the other.

His face as it clears each popping wave –
his eyes –
how unsure where he is.

OLDER AUNT

The older aunt never swam, didn't
even toe the water's edge. Instead

she fingered cuttings at the old kitchen sink,
geranium roots, pale febrile phlox;
unnamed translucencies, gummy stalks,
unsteady heads.

Untangled their hairs,
                pulled their tendrils apart.

                Everyone else in the lake,
she'd be busy with slips, fingernails coaxing
filaments to let filaments go.
Carried scissors in the skirts of her dress.

Daily she turned each jam jar, each juice glass,
incubators, to face into the afternoon sun.
It lit up the stems, emerald smears,
everything slippery as eels.

No one could say exactly why
she refused to enter the lake.

She had her garden to tend: thirteen jars on the sill,
uprooted things, afternoon sun fierce in the afternoon sky.

TREADING WATER

        Spread your arms
as though you could fly.
Darning needles zigzag,
their veined wings
stitch the lake to the sky.
Water, warm as apricots.
Long grasses phantom the lake's unfathomable depths,
plumb lines of weed.

Moted light shoots up from below,
luciferin,
the colour, up close, between cedar bark and ale,
between weak tea
and pale liquid gold.
The scent of the water is the scent of green tea,
or camomile, slightly off.

Sun grips your bare shoulders.
Your forearms, held over-long in the water,
start to dissolve,
turn into lake.

UNCLE BOBBY

Bobby grew up into a boy.
Wrong decade. He
left for the War, Second World,
returning years later,
a box-camera snapshot in hand:
foot soldiers, himself and four friends
lined up in front of a broken-down fence.
Boys drowning in greatcoats.

At the cottage Bobby slept in a cot on the screened-in veranda,
half in, half out of the house.
Old army blanket, and all night
the wind off the shore raked his hair.

Mornings, he'd sprawl
on the wharf or sit in a lawn chair,
slathered in baby oil,
              remembering what?
His fiancée married while
he was at war. He never did.

Later – the house finally his – he glassed in the porch,
wintered in his red velvet chair,
cradling the snapshot: five soldiers, all boys,
in the palm of his hand.

TO OKA

Once to Oka in a rowboat all of you   once
with a ten-horse-power outboard
attached to the back   your uncle

yanks the cord   yanks the cord
steers   his eye on the faraway shore

              the two aunts
on the long middle bench bicker
under sun hats made of pink straw

              your mother
guards the towels in her lap and a box
of marshmallow cookies
a carton of drinks at her feet

              and your father
strangely in the boat too   watches
the water fill the boat's bottom
scoops and bails
              scoops and bails

you and your sister   two-headed bowsprit
dogs in an open-air car
almost barking for speed
and for danger

something lurking   the Loch Ness
the waves smashing   the boat's low
wooden sides   pitching and yawing
half-way   the motor starts coughing
almost capsizing   this rowboat
especially unsuited for deep-water crossings

                                             the lake gullies
ditches and peaks   the boat plunges   bangs
flat on the water   no one speaks
this family   ill-equipped
to endure overlong

                              finally Oka
showing itself
the clear promised land   closer
father bailing   the small plastic pail
still in his grip
scooping   scraping the bottom
uncle squinting now under his baby-oiled brow
aunts in a scowl
mother   mouth folded
the towels bunched in her lap

                          ever-present
especially near shore   the danger
something like anger

a strong chance of rocks

HOW BELONG

Sleeves of worker bees harvest your arms.
You are not sweet;
you only want to belong.

The river runs in; there
crossings are made. The river runs
in greys and in browns. Some days

an inky-blue paisleys the brown;
the lake, drenched in places
by sky, shot silk.

Bees busy your neck. They sing
into your ears. Untutored,
you cannot decipher what's meant.

Where the river flows in, the gap
enters history, the opening
where sun collapses from day.

Though you know nothing
of bee song or currents, *lac maternal*
does not let you drown.

HOW MEND THE YEARS

        let him sit on the beach
my uncle   in his lawn chair
that folds like a stork
aluminum and shredded
blue webbing   glass of Labatts
in his hand

          let him unreel
the past on the waves   psalms
pastures and lilies
the cosmos blooming   stargazing
a blur he almost can feel   made one
with what he is seeing   lake
and the line between water and sky

let him hum without tune
he spools thin lines of bliss
as if fishing
hitching this place to the quiet
promise of peace   geography's
comforting shape
this bluish-brown water   this meniscus
parasol sky   moving   unmoving
unhurried as pre-historical time
let him memorize
the lake's surface   find

in what he sees there
something that mends

ANGELWINGS

their obsidian shine
streaks the night window
rectangular   single-paned

inside the house nothing moves

the oak   its leaves gloved shadows
leans on the house
slants it into the sand

FRÈRE GABRIEL CROSSES THE LAKE

the clink   his knife on the plate's scraped-up surface   heel of
bread   rind of cheese   pool of red-clover honey   his tread on the
dining-hall boards
                    how he crosses the lake after dark

something heard or imagined   sleight of noise behind the shed
behind the cottage five miles across   dark matter   at dusk the heat
begins to road-rise   door open   door falling closed

how much to believe   leftover sun well past children's bedtime
later   night wind lifting the moon from the waves   crickets   bull-
frogs bigger than bowls   acorns knocking the roof's asphalt tiles

his past is unfrangible   his form unchanging when he sits on the
chapel's pine bench   when he places his morning-pale feet into his
boots to walk to the barn to milk six Jersey cows   when three ma-
son bees light on his brow   even then nothing alters his material
state

silent all day and unseen he lived beyond your child eyes   light-
restricted   the far shore   unaffected by clay or by clouds   holding
his breath   his mother's faith   crossing herself when she knelt to
spread wax on her yellow planked floor   her lips moving

if you say dream   if you conjure what might have been   how much
will stay true   how long   his past hovers in faith   if you think
he was angel   apparition   his own quantum leap   sleepwalker
far from his home   if you saw him once heronwing the broad lake
surface-low   if you add June bugs   a sky-wash of mauve

FRÈRE GABRIEL'S LIFE 1

It begins at 2 a.m., the world still spawning slate, nocturnal paws crick-cracking bush twigs outside the black window. Apples asleep inside their trees; cows still barned. Bees waxing in hives. He raises his body, contemplates its seven complaints. In his small cell. Does he admit the concept: the *cell's* darkened window? Or does his pride swell in such penance? If so, he must contemplate the bare floor. Snapping sounds. Contemplate the truth of this untimely hour. Socks like felted mats. He must pray. To his mother in Laval-des-Rapides, he bows his head. To his father underground, he dispenses his thoughts. To Thomas Merton, he cites each authentic word. He blows on his hands. He strives for *bios aggelikos,* but he is one monk among two hundred. Mistaken prayer, he cannot sheer himself from this life.

FRÈRE GABRIEL'S LIFE 2

God, the Father, fashioned the cosmos from nothing: not dust, not rock, not sand, not bone, not a mother's womb, not spitting into His right hand, not rubbing two sticks together or breathing into an excess of blue-ish green slime. *Rien de rien.* From nothing at all.

Still there are rules. Père Abbot unfolds them one by one. Permitting on Tuesday Frère Jean to visit his consumptive sister in Hull, and Frère Luc to hitch the ruined horse to the flatbed layered with honeycombs, jellies and cheese. Permitting no radio in the dining hall, even the day the new Pope is announced. No eggs except at Christmas, and once a week for Frère Gabriel, the thinnest of Père Abbot's thin tonsured sons.

At confession, Frère Gabriel receives the same penance each time: seven rosaries and five Ways of the Cross, which, as a rule, he completes on his knees.

FRÈRE GABRIEL'S LIFE 3

His own father at night would stoop, rifle through the woodbox to
scoop logs and small splits, lay the morning fire inside the black
stove, crossing one stick over the other into one perfect square,
then stutter to bed up thirteen cold stairs. Each one he would count
– *une, deux, trois* – as he climbed, every night, closer to heaven. One
morning his wife had to carry him, his body, bone-thin, down the
stairs, early May, one by one, unfaltering, just as the birds
began singing.

ARMIES OF FROGS

After Tim Lilburn's "Slow World"

The lake is a woman who no longer
looks in the mirror. She lets her beard bristle,
forced to overhear strangers rowing their boats.
The lake breeds black bass in basements of muck, keeps armies
of frogs in the coves. Sometimes
the lake chokes in her sleep, waking
to bullfrogs, leopard frogs and green frogs.
Leeches, pickerel, northern pike. All her loves
circle her waist. Though no longer
the chorus frogs, whom she laments.

In the middle, Sea-Doos, speedboats, tumble the lake,
carve up the waves. Late July, Montreal halts for two weeks.
Police patrol shorelines.
There's a ferry to Oka all day.

Near the shore, muskrat and foxes.
Female mallards sit in the trees.
Maple keys shrug
at the lake's hem. She no longer keeps track.

Holy water and toxins, black-patent tadpoles
with prominent eyes. Thunderstorms
from the west. Decoys and guns in the fall.

Once, barges for pelts and coniferous logs.
Once, food smuggled on powerboats
for the Mohawk behind the blockade.
Beyond old,
        she turns ragged blue in high wind.

Always heading somewhere downstream:
Lachine, Lac St. Louis, the St. Lawrence,
Montreal. Nearby, bordering the town of Ste.-Anne-de-Bellevue,
Mafiosi inhabit their fortified homes.

Mid-century, the chorus frogs abandoned the lake:
harsh cold, the Seaway, fertilizers, tailings,
a factory upstream. Their skin tinged
a greyish-green tan,
their rapturous piping, utterly lost.

OKA CRISIS

You saw the war start on your sister's TV:
masks and camouflage gear. Before that,
you saw nothing at all.

           Until you knew what it meant,
what could you know? High-school history,
blue textbook, Fathers Brébeuf and Lalemant.
From a distance, five miles or more,
what can be seen?

The lake, a spreading brown water
coming to rest
before it reaches St. Lawrence's olivine rush.
Fattened hinge,
endless trade route, Old World and New.

Two mountains, seen only from the lake's centre.
Wherever centre resides. Absent
from nautical maps, and unnamed.

Island cottages morph into mansions,
mushroom the land.
Islanders don't return to the city when summer ends. Anymore.
When summer ends they book a cruise to Cancun.

The monastery, eclipsed, its functions
                    stripped clean,
is now a shop, old photographs on tourist display,
the classrooms of a private international school.
A funeral home, movie set, bells
with no sound, brambled paths leading down
to the water
catching its breath.

The reservation is a settlement
plus several lots in the town. Owned
by the Feds, purchased
from centuries of history,
Sulpician priests, City Hall.
                    Unceded by Mohawks
who keep living there, who claim it,
time immemorial, claim the pines that secure the small hill,
claim their dead buried under the pines.
                    And the fish,
and the fishing huts that stud winter ice,
racoons and foxes, firewood chopped
from the trees, the narrow main road,
the farms and the horses, the Mohawk Gas station,
eggs, cigarettes, neon lights, warrior flags,
hand-painted signs.

The Oka Crisis was a war:
concussion grenades, AK-47s,
barricades, tripwires, three months
of mid-summer heat. One man died.
More were beaten, beaten down.
                      Long-standing tombstones,
golf course expansion,
who owns the land,
what was taken, which priests, who owns
the trees. Nation to nation.

One hundred years ago, the Oka Church
burned to the ground. No one knows who.

Twenty years ago, police raided the pines.
History—lake or rapids, seen or unseen—
rivers on. Police cruisers, bulletproof
vests, warrior code names, the army called in.
No one knows how hate works. No one knows
why the Mohawk
don't own the land. No one knows
who shot Corporal Marcel Lemay.
Morning,
                the sweet grass was still burning.
Smoke started to rise.
The S.Q. – sudden tear gas,
grenades. The wind changed directions,
the bullet stole
through his bulletproof vest.

NORTHERN GATE

The northern gate, opening into,
and out,
into moving away
the day you drive through,
the wrong day: shining blades, territorial
leaves, apples unready, jade walnuts on trees.

No one walks on the road. No one drives.
The hour is wrong, or the road.
Just ragged clouds blowing all over the sky
and a hawk canting. *Kanesatake.*
So much green you begin to crave
crimson silk, unravelling, want to be
somewhere else. Shame, your shame is being in the wrong place.
No one waits for you at the corner.

Rain, one by one, on the windscreen.
At the gas station, one man, head down
as he fills his tank.
No one gazes from windows,
no windows seen. Houses
guard the far ends of driveways.
Wind wails a warning. Shame is
the failure to belong sufficiently to what is beloved.
Northern gate, opening into,
and out.

L'ÎLE-CADIEUX

The narrow island feathers the lake,
pinioned, points to the east. Scallop-edged,
its rachis is paved
end to end; its quill forms
a short iron bridge.

Those who live on the island
survey the lake's changeable face,
theatre of water and sky.
They live among deciduous trees
growing down into the lake.
Maples' thick leaves move the shadows. Sumac
tropicate near the bridge,
red velvet torches, green parrot fronds.
Beeches with pachyderm bark.

The small pinnated island lies light
on the water. Those who live there
know worry: the lake's currents
and the whipped rivers of air.
They pray that the trees, their deep roots,
will fasten, keep this feather of land
from lifting into the wind.

WALKING THE ISLAND ROAD AFTER DINNER

Walking the narrow raised road
under the wings
of your parents, father starting
to whistle, freed from the house
of the sisters-in-law, blackbird
with hands in his pockets,
mother in polished tan cotton shorts,
house sparrow, wings folded
under her soft blousy wrap.
Asking nothing.
What were their thoughts? You

are content just to stroll
with them,
hover close to their silky coverts.

    Sometimes you stop
to burst the orangey weed-flowers,
tap them or blow, seed after seed
arcing onto the road. You and your sister
seeding the road. Asking nothing:
not the name of the flowers,
or the tune or the time.
      Or how
your parents kept hidden
their back-mounted wings.

FRÈRE GABRIEL'S LIFE 4

It is penance. No meat. No speech. No guest who's not family.
No book that's not God's. No choice that is not Père Abbot's. No fish unless sick. In winter frost thickens the windows and walls. Bed at seven like children. Up at two when night still blinds the cold panes and the bells begin clanging. Kneel then, head heavy with hood. Nine offices, each with its own special bell. At least nine kinds of work, each a penance. Milking in shadowy stalls, hardly seeing cow or the pail. Filing out to break stones big as beds. Pulling weeds, haying fields filled with sun. Hay dust swarms the barn. Inside, mopping floors, the refectory stagnant with beans, cabbage soup. Dipping candles, stitching stiff boots. Idle hands cradle demons. Even the silence is thick with merciless sounds: Frère Marcel wheezing through Mass; Frère Jean smacking his lips through each meal. Offering these up. Each penance wings a soul past the stone walls to rest in the willows that weep on the shore.

FRÈRE GABRIEL'S LIFE 5

His chewed-up lips. His hands like spades under loose sleeves. How he allows what happens each day. Permits sun to bake his pink, freckled brow. Allows Frère Martin to nudge him at Mass, eyelids shut tight as freshwater clams. How long this monk kneels. His slow gait, his impossible pace, the way he places his fork on the plate. Carefully lifts his light voice in high praise, stills his lips when in prayer. It is not so much that Frère Gabriel talks to God; every monk does. But that God talks to him.

WHEN HEAT FALLS

Mid-summer, the lake stares down the sun and the sky,
what was once thought of
as heaven.
A hot lazy raft rocks its complaints twenty feet from shore.
In the afternoon haze sadness
loses all definition. The sun
is another country, a martyrdom
of touch.
                    At forty-five degrees
the air congeals, props up trees,
human bodies, houses, erratic stones.

The heat lowers
onto the lake's lassitude,
its small worn-out wrinkles.
                        It hardly breathes.
Fish bloat on the surface, loll their bellies,
wash ashore, pallid, appear,
disappear between rocks.

The lake prays to Oka's two highest hills,
their rolling loft, unseen from the south.

June bugs pierce the dazed hearing world.
Words abandon flesh. Chokecherries,
reeds, milkweed froth the lake's shore.

The shoreline slowly recedes,
beginning to shrink, the lake rising
in droplets, almost nothingness,
on its way into the sky.

CARDINALS, CROWS

Hear them piping one by one:
we are here, we are here.
Cardinal solos –
suns behind clouds,
almost papal.
Look up: each too divine
to appear.

Crows do not hide. They are
medieval friars selling indulgences,
safe passages, relics they lift from the eaves.
Holy cards, greased bones, bottle caps.
Crow tricks –
everything is at risk.

Holy, profane,
hidden, in plain sight –
the end of the world
will arrive
in the mouth of a bird.

LAKE 2

drawing cowls of quiet around uncertain space sinking through pebbles and coarse grains of sand no sound it spreads into grass lies flat for seasons timeless hovering even at shore a presentiment a mirage shape-shifting mesmer holding the surrounding rocks in place through reverence alone the air above claims no geography the lake needs nothing but river's brown mouth solitary quiet as the dragonfly that quilts nimbussed gloss as the eel that ribbons the squelch as unlit fish surveying beneath cirrussed weeds   even when shirred when breezes scoop atoms of foam even when the world slants with rain and with wind the lake won't complain white noise alone nothing the ear can locate even in early morning when heron spears frog no sound will ring out

GHOSTS MOVING IN FORESTED SHADE

light through the low woods
unbinds clavicle   soles
trompe l'oeil
deciduous shadow and shudder
quiver with unabashed shine

what is fixed in the truth is in flux
sleights the eye   there is goodness
there are ghosts moving
faster than wind   through low bush and leaves
they move more surely than light

SUMMER ENDS

mist then   as August tapers
to September   lifts
the lake's surfeit heat

night chills the breakfast milk
oak leaves still frill
the kaleidoscoped sky

the mist slips off by ten
no one has died yet
no one swims until noon

no one speaks of the end
leaf   water   child

THINGS CHANGE

a bird keening in flight
the shape of a marsh hawk   shadow
with malevolent wings

the lake is benign now   steadfast
why imagine it flying away
small mammal heart
in its beak

LAST DAY

    Variation on a glosa – Archibald Lampman's "Thunderstorm"

toss in the windrack up the muttering wind
the leaves hang still above the weird twilight
the hurrying centres of the storm unite

an afternoon rain
starts without enough
warning   though
to be honest you carry
a borrowed umbrella
            walk the road
for the last time   above you
the leaves toss in the windrack
up the muttering sky

the sky takes on rubbings
of charcoal   rain-
patter paces your steps
but still you will not
turn back   the umbrella
staves off the worsening wet
at roadside the leaves
hang still
        in the weird light

you race rain for the cottage
where you lived as a child
quirk of the storm   sluicing you
onto this particular porch

side door locked
new owners away   you brace
the umbrella's inadequate shield
wind shoves
against you   rain streams
down your cheeks
directly upon you
the hurrying
centres of the storm unite

MONASTIC LIFE 7

It is gone. The last twenty monks left in a bus for a house somewhere north. Praise songs no longer climb the white pines. Prayers no longer smoke evening skies. No monk bows south to the lake or beats his gaunt breast for trespasses past. No confessions within the scent of the shore. No sheep in the barns. No apiary, no fat-sided bees. Only apples hang heavy from branches – and fall.

Night galloped through cloisters, cracked stones from the walls, trampled gardens of lavender and mint. Once, two hundred obeyed their vocations or their own mother's hearts. So many chants. So many white robes. In their small well-waxed cells, devotions and the splitting of hypothetical hairs. So much cider; there was honey and cream.

MONASTIC LAKE

Liturgical in its way, the lake unfolds, arising in wavelets in morning, changing with weather or time of day, without evidence of sorrow or blame. The water claims nothing for itself. Without hue or clear shape, it allows what gathers around it – air's blue, palimpsests of horsetail in flight. Mud washes in from the Ottawa's tongue, silting through. Summer sun beats the water to bronze. Where rocks curve, the lake bends. It sinks to its depths, evaporates or floods according to season and year. Even its storms bequeath hush. Scent of fish dying, algal bloom, clams broken on shore. Anything that passes through is transformed. Who watches, finally revealed. How self submerges itself, metaphor for mystery, drowning, escape.

WHAT'S UNDER

fish down there   tadpoles   smallmouth bass
red-eyed   bicycle tires   musky pike
walleye and drum
a fishing hut that fell through the ice four years ago
three cases of beer   the owner out for a leak
made it to shore

perch   sunfish   catfish   rosary beads   bibles
carp   bullets   the sturgeon finally returned
they bump around in the murk
nose a ten-horsepower motor
a rotary phone

garpike down there and minnows in shallows
risking jars and small nets
minnows like sudden cartoons

the neighbour fishes
but not through the ice
wood ducks in spring   dabble
feet paddle the water
mallards all summer long   tipping up
going down

EIGHT MILES TO THE CENTRE

You watch how water accommodates wind,
how the lake turns direction, curls
its lips white, turns colour, almost

opaque, from root-brown to light nickel-grey,
textured and fringed, turns its mind
to the shore.

In the middle of things
you've been given a place.
Eight miles to the centre.

What difference if the lake changes –
or if you belong? This water,
this spring-flooded land, cannot happen

in exile. The lake you are left with:
algae, neon-lime silk, skeins of it, spun
out of nowhere, untroubled cumulus blooms.

SUN GOING DOWN

Nine o'clock, the hour of the sun
going down, listing to the south.
The drowsing dark lake
shushes itself on the shore.
Divinity lingering this way.

Nine o'clock, the hour of fox
on the move. Hour of closing,
the sky closing over,
heat losing its hold.

Fox stealing slow
as the sun,
        going down
to the shore,
looking for fish.

ACKNOWLEDGEMENTS

Many thanks to Lorna Crozier, my caring and exacting MFA supervisor, who encouraged and guided *Lake of Two Mountains* from its inception. Without her, this project simply would not have been realized. Appreciation also to other members of the University of Victoria's Creative Writing Department, both fellow students and faculty, especially Tim Lilburn and John Barton. Much gratitude to Sue Chenette, my very thoughtful editor, who helped to shape the final version. To my sister, Donna Sharkey, who understands the childhood experience of the Lake better than anyone I know, many thanks for being there. Thanks to the people of L'Île-Cadieux, especially the mayor, his wife and the town's secretary for their efforts to find accommodation for me; Pat for her friendship; and Lucille and Francois for their hospitality. And always, enduring gratefulness to Chris Fox, my companion and first reader for so many years.

Thanks also to Ursula Vaira of Leaf Press, editor of the chapbook anthology, *What Else Could I Dare to Say*, where "Whether Wind" first appeared.

ARLEEN PARÉ is a poet and novelist with an MFA in Creative Writing from the University of Victoria. Her first book, *Paper Trail*, won the Victoria Butler Book Prize and was a finalist for the Dorothy Livesay B.C. Book Award for Poetry. Her second book was a mixed-genre novel entitled *Leaving Now*. Paré's writing has appeared in several Canadian literary journals and anthologies. Originally from Montreal, she lived for many years in Vancouver, where she worked as a social worker and administrator to provide community housing for people with mental illnesses. She now lives in Victoria with her partner, Chris Fox.